Memoirs of a Broken Vessel

Linda Coleman

Dallas, Texas

Memoirs of a Broken Vessel: *Experience Freedom and Transformation* by Linda Coleman

Higgins Publishing | www.higginspublishing.com - The publisher is not responsible for websites (or their content) that are not owned by the publisher. Higgins Publishing is committed to excellence in the publishing industry. The company reflects the philosophy established by the founder, based on Psalm 68:11, 'The Lord gave the word, and great was the company of those who published it.'

Library of Congress Control Number: 2021910102

Coleman, Linda – Memoirs of a Broken Vessel: *Experience Freedom and Transformation*

Higgins Publishing First Softback Edition   August 2021

Includes Index pcm Pages 82

English: 978-1-941580-20-2 (SB) 978-1-941580-21-9 (EB)

REL012000   RELIGION / Christian Living / General
REL012120   RELIGION / Christian Living / Spiritual Growth

For information about special discounts for bulk purchases, subsidiary, foreign and translations rights & permissions, please contact Higgins Publishing at sales@higginspublishing.com.

DEDICATION

The Call and Destined Purpose Jeremiah 1:4-5

"Then the word of the Lord came unto me, saying, Before I formed thee in the belly I knew thee; and before thou camest forth out of the womb I sanctified thee, and I ordained thee a prophet unto the nations."

This book belongs to my heavenly Father, Lord and Savior Jesus Christ.

Because of you, Lord, I am called, destined, and purposed. Purposed for greatness. I answer the call and walk in obedience to your beckoning. Here I am, Lord. Here I am.

I made good on writing this book for you, Lord. This is my story. This is your book. I deliver my soul, Lord. I have obeyed your voice to write!

Thank you, Lord. It is finished! Amen.

Linda Coleman

TABLE OF CONTENTS

INTRODUCTION

This book is the true story of my life. It will encourage and enlighten you in ways that you may never have imagined. Starting with my earliest, innocent years, it details the good times winding through areas of mistakes and memories to the present day. As you read this book, you will no doubt be touched by my life changing testimonies and my life's precarious twists and turns. Its intriguingly explicit content will amaze and stir you to take a deeper look into who you are and intend to become. Enjoy the ride!

CHAPTER 1
THE BEGINNING

I am a New Year's Day baby. My earliest memory is that of an eager three-year-old girl in the kitchen with Mom and Dad. Mom was telling Dad that she was going out to do something and would return shortly. Dad began to wash dishes. I asked Dad if I could help him. He pulled up a chair and let me stand in the chair to wash a dish. After that he said that I had done enough and took me down. I was so proud that I had helped Dad. I could not wait until Mom got back so that I could tell her that I had washed dishes. Mom came right back as she said she would, and Dad told her that I wanted to help him wash dishes, and I had washed a dish. We lived in a two-story white frame house in the 3600 block of Colonial

Street in South Dallas. My grandmother, Odessa Woods, lived with us. My grandmother was old and sickly. I remember the day my grandmother died. Mom called for an ambulance and Grandmother passed away.

I have fun memories of catching the train at Reunion Station in downtown Dallas with Mom and Aunt Evelyn. Back then we would commute back and forth between Dallas and San Antonio, TX. Our family had military men, Air Force and Army. My dad was an Air Force policeman. Dad and Uncle Morris were stationed at Randolph Air Force Base. Uncle Doug was in the Army. I was born at Lackland Air Force Base Hospital. Our family would also commute back and forth from Dallas to San Antonio by car. I remember riding in my Uncle Doug's car back then. I believe it was a 1954 Ford. We would stop at the back of a store to get food and use the restroom. Back in those days, colored people were not allowed to go into the front of the establishment. Those were such fond memories. I remember attending Colonial Elementary School in the first grade and TC Haskell Elementary School in the second grade.

I remember troubled times. There was a side of Dad that was gentle and kind. I loved my dad, and he loved me! I was his little, precious love. Mother was the Queen. She held it all together. The family had struggles. We moved a lot. Our family lived on Fourth Ave in South Dallas near the Fair Park. Dad worked for the Coca Cola Bottling Company at one time.

That time of my life was so special! The State Fair of Texas was just a few streets over. State Fair times were great. I was just a young girl. We always knew when it was fair time because the weather would change. It would become cold, wet, and dreary. We had to put on coats and dress warm due to the weather change. It was fair time! Mom did not like going to the fair, but my dad always took me to the fair! What a great time and great memories. Memories of Dad and other neighbors parking cars in the yard to make money so that people could attend the State Fair was a big thing at that time. Those were the days! Our family moved back to San Antonio and lived in the East Terrace Court housing projects. My brother Vincent and I attended Riley Junior High School. It was the elementary side of Riley Junior

High in 1962-63. My cousins Beverly and Brenda also attended Riley Junior High School. I recall the day that President John Kennedy was assassinated. We were at school that day. We got the news of his shooting and school was dismissed. Everyone was devastated. It was a cold dreary incredibly quiet and somber dark day in and around the world.

I loved it when my grandmother Marie Coleman, Dad's mother, came to visit with us to attend the Pentecostal convention. She would take me with her to the convention. I loved it! We had wonderful grandparents. My beautiful grandparents, Dad's parents, Levi and Marie Coleman, were awesome grandparents and always showed love in words and deeds to us. My precious Aunt Edna also visited us in San Antonio, she is Dad's sister.

One thing I remember about my dad was that he had beautiful penmanship and was an artist. He could draw beautiful pictures. I remember him sending off to submit his drawings to be rated, and they were accepted. Dad drew a picture of Mom. It was beautiful. Things were not always peachy cream with the marriage. Nonetheless, our parents loved us. I remember attending Dorrie Miller Elementary

School. We moved back to Dallas when I was 12 years old. Mom bought us back to Dallas, and we stayed with uncle Doug and Aunt Faye, Mom's baby sister. We lived with them for a while until Mom could find housing. I attended John Neely Brown Elementary School in the sixth grade. One of my fondest memories was the day when we visited the historical Miller More Mansion. This was the home of William Brown Miller who served in the Confederate Army. It was located across the street from the school. The mansion was going to be relocated to the Dallas Heritage Village in downtown Dallas. It was an awesome occasion and will always be a great memory of mine. I attended Oliver Wendell Holmes Middle School my seventh grade year. We were blessed to get an apartment in the Bracken Ridge housing projects on Monaghan Court. This was our first apartment with our Mom in Dallas. I attended Franklin Delano Roosevelt High School from the 8th through the 12th grade. When I turned 16, Mom gave me a birthday party. She bought me a stereo record player for my birthday. I had my first boyfriend at 16. I dated other guys in high school. I had family in Washington, D.C. My siblings and I went to D.C. to visit for the first time in 1971.

CHAPTER 2

BECOMING AN ADULT

I was an A-B student at Roosevelt High School and graduated in the National Honor Society. I graduated in the 1972 graduating class of Roosevelt High School. After graduation, I went to stay in Washington, D.C. with my Aunt Evelyn and my cousins Beverly and Brenda. During my stay in D.C., I met my first child's father. I was pregnant at 18. I went back home to live with my parents. I gave birth to my first child. I had a beautiful baby boy. I was now a young single mother. Things did not work out with my son's father and myself. I had become a mother at 19. I was always a smart young lady. I got on food stamps, but I vowed to myself that I would not be a person receiving government assistance all my life. I felt that I had made a mistake by getting pregnant and not being married. The Lord had a conversation with me which made me want to choose better for myself and my child. So, I vowed that I would not have any more children without being married. God honored the choice that I made. He sent me a husband.

I started working at a department store in downtown Dallas. The name of that department store was Titche Goettinger. I worked in the credit department. One day I was walking in the corridors of the department store. Along the way a handsome young man saw me and got my attention. He saw me again in passing and stopped me and asked me for my phone number. This is how my journey to becoming a wife began. My husband and I were both 19 years old. He called me and invited me out. He took me to a movie. The movie *The Exorcist* was out at that time. My Lord! What a movie! He fell in love with me, and I with him. Before long we were married! In December of 1974, I was a wife. I was 19 years old, and my husband turned 20. We were blessed with our first son. He was an 8 month baby. He came early. My husband and I were in love and became young parents. I asked my husband if he wanted to name our son junior. He said no, that he did not want to name our son junior.

Our marriage was not perfect; we fought and argued a lot. One day my husband and I fought. I was fed up with the fighting at this point. I went into the room where my two boys were. I gathered their clothes and a few other things and went to my mother's house. At this point, enough was enough. I told my mother to call my Aunt Evelyn or somebody. I had to get out of Dallas!

CHAPTER 3

THE TRANSFORMATION

A New Journey into a New Life Begins

My mother contacted my Aunt Evelyn. Aunt Evelyn sent tickets for me and my boys to come stay with her in Washington, D.C. I never said goodbye to my husband. I just left.

I took my flight on Braniff Airlines with my two small boys. I remember how nice the flight was and being served a genuinely nice meal. I had my first ever Cornish hen meal stuffed with wild rice and sides. I remember cutting into the Cornish hen and the juices and wild rice were quite tantalizing. The meal was delicious. I was extremely impressed as I never had this meal before. We arrived in Washington, D.C., and I was taken to my cousin's apartment. Being in D.C. awakened memories of having met my first son's dad. We had not seen or spoken to each other for some time. My son was two years old at that time. My youngest son was just a baby. Fate would have it that shortly after arriving to my cousin's apartment she told me that she had seen my son's father a few hours before I arrived. This had to be a meeting of fate because my cousin had not seen or talked to him since I left D.C. My cousin said that he had given her his phone number, so I was able to contact him. I called him and arranged to meet him. My son's father saw his child for the first time. My son's father and I started spending time together. He had two other sons that he brought with him, and his three sons played together. There was a time when he took me to meet his mother.

His mother and I talked about my situation and my heartfelt disappointment with my life at this point.

I took my boys home to Dallas to stay with my mother.

I was at a point of deep despair. I felt that I had failed in life and just did not know what to do. I walked down the street toward my Aunt Evelyn's apartment with a sad countenance. I felt hopeless. I felt that I had totally failed at this thing called life. The question was, what is left to do now? A failed relationship, a rocky marriage. Dear God! Dear God! Help, Lord!

I went into the apartment. My aunt was at work. I stood in the dining room and prayed.

I had thought of people in Dallas that were saved and lived a holy life. I was so disappointed with my life, the choices that I had made, and the mistakes that I had made. This was it. I had come to a crossroad. Desperate, alone, and feeling hopeless, I had to decide what to do going forward. I prayed! Lord Jesus, I know that there is a such thing as being saved. Lord, save me!

Instantly, I was saved! Changed! Romans 10:13, "For whosoever shall call upon the name of the Lord shall be saved." 1ˢᵗ Corinthians 5:17, "Therefore if any man be in Christ, he is a new creature; old things are passed away; behold, all things are become new." I was changed! I had become a "new creature in Christ." I had been given a new life. A changed life. My sins had been forgiven and cast into the sea of forgiveness, no longer to be remembered or held against me.

This time of transformation and transition from sinner to saint was so unexpected. There was no planning or foreseeing it. It just happened! I was not in a church. There was no pastor, preacher, or spiritual person there. It was just me and Jesus. I was born again. I did not understand what was happening to me. There was no one to explain it. There were times I thought that I was losing my mind. I was saved at age 22. My aunt and family saw the change that I had experienced. My Aunt Evelyn took me to a church service one night. We sat on the first row. The musicians began to play skillfully on the instruments. In an instant I was up dancing in the spirit! I had never done that before in my life. I came to myself and sat down. I asked my aunt did you see that? She said yes! Now in the Baptist church, I had seen people "get happy" but that had never happened to me until that special night. One lady commented to me that I was glowing.

I knew that holiness people were different. They dressed different meaning no make-up, no earrings, no pants, all of which I wore. I had to change! The Midi/Maxi look of the 70's was in at that time. I changed my attire. No more pants, earrings, or make-up for me, although I kept one pair of green pants, just in case. I was now saved! I had started going to church often. I was trying to find out about this new way of life. One day a church lady told me that a member of her family had gotten the Holy Ghost and was speaking in other tongues and that she was seeking God to get it. I did not have a clue what she was talking about. I had never heard of such a thing.

One day my aunt who worked at a jewelry store offered to pierce my ears. I was so excited and agreed because they had never been pierced before. I always was afraid to have them pierced. So, the day came, and I went to the jewelry store and had them pierced. They put the string in and after a while some small earrings. My aunt told me that when the time came after they were healed that she would buy me some cross earrings to put in my ears. The day came, and my aunt gave me the cross earrings to put in my ears. They were beautiful! The Holy Spirit chastened me. The Holy Spirit sorely reproved me with a harsh and sore reproof. He spoke to me and said, "Anoint your ears with oil! Thou shalt not pierce the

Lord's body." I cried trembling with fear and obeyed the Lord's voice. I told my aunt what the Lord said to me. My aunt never said another word. She took the earrings back and that was that.

I experienced a presence that would come in the room when I would read my Bible at home. I did not know what it was but was afraid of it and would put away my Bible when it would present itself. One day my child's father came by. I was reading my Bible that day. He asked me why I was reading the Bible. He told me with a stern reprimand, "Man wrote the Bible and not God!" Well silly me decided that I would put away my Bible and not read it anymore. Oh, what a mistake that was! The next day I was chastised of the Lord. He was angry with me for my decision not to read His Word. I experienced what was a haze to come over my mind. It was like God had dulled my senses. I began to see things in a fog and hear things in a muffle. I was afraid. I feared for my life. I laid down that night with the Bible in my chest next to my heart and hoped that I would see tomorrow.

The next day when I was awakened, the light of day lightly beamed through the shades at the window. I did not get out of the bed. I slid out of bed down to my knees and sorely wept before the Lord with all my heart! I was so glad to be alive and to see another day! I totally surrendered to Him. I gave Him all of me! Suddenly, I felt a change. This language, a new language was coming out of my mouth. I was speaking in another language that I had not ever spoken and could not control. I got up and walked through the apartment speaking in other tongues as the Spirit gave utterance! I had received the baptism of the Holy Ghost! Just as Acts 2 states, "1) And when the day of Pentecost was fully come, they were all with one accord in one place. 2) and suddenly there came a sound from heaven as of a rushing mighty wind, and it filled all the house where they were sitting. 3) and there appeared unto them cloven tongues like as of fire, and it sat upon each of them. 4) and they were all filled with the Holy Ghost, and began to speak with other tongues, as the Spirit gave them utterance." I backslid shortly after receiving the Holy Ghost. I needed to be taught how to keep the victory.

One day our neighbor, I will call her Charlotte, from downstairs, asked me if I would ride with her to North

Carolina. I agreed to ride with her. I had given up all my pants except one pair of green pants, earrings, and makeup and all the worldly things. I convinced myself that I could not ride out of town in a dress or skirt. I put on my pants and off we went to North Carolina. We went to a family member's house first, where we would stay while we were there. We left there so that Charlotte could take care of some business. Shortly we arrived at Charlotte's aunt's house where she asked me to stay for a short while until she finished her business. I agreed. As soon as she left, her aunt went and got this great big Bible and went to the scripture in Deuteronomy 22:5, "A woman shall not wear that which pertaineth unto man, neither shall a man put on a woman's garment: for all that do so are abomination unto the Lord thy God." I was reproved. I was shocked, to say the least. The Lord had followed me all the way to North Carolina to reprove me of those pants! I told the lady that I knew better and that I had just made an excuse for myself to wear those pants one more time. I told her that just as soon as I got back to the house, that I would get out of them and not wear them again.

We returned to D.C., and I had such a longing for my family. I really missed my husband and my boys. I had taken my boys back home earlier for my mother to keep. I was so sad. I missed being a wife. I missed having a husband and married life. My heart was broken. I longed for my husband. I remember asking God why it was so hard to live life in this world. I cried out to God in my despair and anguish. I started to feel a heavy pain in my chest. The pain was a crushing pain with much pressure. It was as though God had taken hold of my heart and was squeezing the life out of me. I cried out to Him and exclaimed that I did not want to die! I said, "Lord, I do not want to leave my boys!" I told Him that I knew that I had a good mother, but I felt that she could not take care of them the way that I could because they were my boys. The pain subsided.

CHAPTER 4

VISIONS, DREAMS, AND MIRACLES.

This chapter is my recollection of some of the visions, dreams, and miracles and other things that I have experienced.

1ˢᵗ Vison. One day while in Aunt Evelyn's living room, the Lord came to me in a vision. He spoke to me and told me to hold out my hands. I held out my hands, and he began to put promises into my hands. He called them out to me one by one. Then He went away.

Illumination of God's Word

One day as I was reading my Bible, the Lord spoke to me. He instructed me to pick up my Bible. He took me to a scripture in the Bible. The passage in the Bible where

He called my attention to lit up on the page. He illuminated the Word on the page of the Bible to me. I had never experienced the actual illumination of God's Word before!

1st Miracle. My Moment of Salvation (Conversion). I stood in my aunt's dining room and began to talk to the Lord. I remember saying to Him, "Lord, I know there is a thing as being saved. Lord, save me!" Instantly I was transformed into a new creature! Old things have passed away, and all things became new! Everything looked different to me. My hands looked new, the grass looked greener, the sky looked bluer, and the world appeared to have taken on a new essence of significance. I remember going through the apartment screaming, "Thank you, Jesus! Thank you, Jesus! Thank you, Jesus!" I screamed from the top of my lungs. I was so thankful! The Lord had saved me! I was a new creature!

2nd Miracle. Infilling of the Holy Ghost. I was filled with the Holy Ghost in my aunt's living room with the evidence of speaking in other tongues as the Spirit gave utterance. I called this my Pentecost experience.

CHAPTER 5

THE DEPARTMENT STORE INCIDENT

I was working in a department store while staying with Aunt Evelyn. One day an incredibly unique thing happened to me. I was a baby saint with childlike faith. I had a lot of zeal. I had been reading my Bible and read about how Jesus had healed the sick. I believed that Jesus could heal the sick, if you believed, and if I prayed for you, you would be healed. I was working on the floor of the department store, and as people came near me, I would ask them if I could pray for them. People would say yes to me praying for them, and I did. A lady came into the store with many large protruding lumps on her body. She used a walker to help herself walk. I saw her and approached her. I asked her, "Do you believe in

Jesus? Do you believe that He is a healer?" The lady responded yes to my questions. I asked her if I could pray for her. I laid my hands on her and began to command healing to her body in the name of Jesus. I asked her if she believed in the power of prayer that I had prayed. She said yes and walked away. Well, right after I prayed for her, I begin to feel this heavy presence of a spirit around me and on me. I immediately recognized it to be a demon spirit trying to invade me. I went to the area of the store where the employees were only to go. I would carry a small Bible and cross necklace around my neck. I grabbed my Bible and held it close to me. I held onto my cross necklace. I began to pray and plead the blood of Jesus. The spirit left and went away.

1st Healing at Church

My 2-year-old son had pneumonia. Time after time I had to take him to Children's Medical Center Dallas. I took my son to church. When the call for prayer was made, I took him down. The pastor laid hands on my son that night. He was healed! The condition left him and plagued him no more!

2nd Miracle of Healing at Church

My children were birthed awfully close together. I remember that after giving birth to one of them, I developed a condition that felt like my teeth were very loose in my gums. The pain was very intense. I was sitting in a service one night when the pastor began to preach. I remember that he went to Ephesians 3:20, "Now unto him that is able to do exceedingly abundantly above all that we ask or think, according to the power that worketh in us." Instantly, as those words left his mouth, I felt the healing virtue of God come upon me and healed the condition that plagued me! I suffered with that condition no more. The pastor called for testimonies. I went down and gave my testimony to the glory of God!

CHAPTER 6

THE DREAM

One day while at home with my children, I was expecting at this time, I experienced my first dream. I was home with my children, who were small. I was doing my normal routine of cleaning, folding clothes, and ironing as the children slept. I became very sleepy, which was very unusual for me. I fell into an unconscious state. I begin to dream a dream about being in church. The pastor was preaching a message of hellfire and brimstone. The pastor continued to preach. He began to strike matches that he threw into the crowd. One of the matches that he threw into the crowd fell into my mother's hair. My mother's hair was on fire. I could see the flames burning in her hair. She started to pat her head to put the fire out. I wakened from the dream. The dream frightened me, so I called my first lady and told her about the dream. The first lady instructed me to tell Mother about the dream. Mother came home from work, and I told her about the dream. We went to church that night, and my mother went to the altar to repent.

Ovarian Cyst Disappears! A Miraculous Healing

At age 47, I started to go through perimenopause. During this time, a woman's body makes the natural transition to menopause, marking the end of the reproductive years. Oh my God! I had never experienced anything so drastic as this in my life. During this time in my life I experienced going to the hospital many times. During one of my early ER visits, a pelvic sonogram was ordered. A large pelvic mass was found on my uterus. I was put on medication to stop excessive bleeding and given many options such as hysterectomy to rectify the condition that I suffered. I refused to have a hysterectomy and chose another treatment option. Just as the woman in the Bible, I became a woman with the issue of blood. Yes, I suffered many things at the hands of the doctors. There were many doctor's visits for examinations. I remember having gone to church for prayer for this condition. It was so scary having to go through this awful time in my life. I remember doing one of my many OB/GYN clinic visits the nurse told me that there is life after this. I thanked her for such comforting words. I am a woman of faith. My many years of being saved had taught me to trust God in my situations in life. The doctors kept looking for the mass. The cyst was on my uterus.

Again, I experienced excessive bleeding. Blood flowed as an opened faucet. I called the ambulance and was taken to the ER at a local hospital. After examination, the doctor told me that my uterus was normal. She told me that she was sending me for another pelvic sonogram. I went for the appointment to have the sonogram. The technician asked me, "What did you do? Where did you go?" I responded that I went to Jesus! I went to my scheduled doctor's visit to have the sonogram read. The doctors told me that sonogram was normal and that they would see me in a year! I give glory to God. I was healed by the power of God! Jehovah Rapha, "The Lord who heals."

CHAPTER 7

UNEXPECTED MIRACLE

I returned home to Dallas. My husband and I had reunited. I longed for the presence of the Lord and began to seek out churches to attend to be restored in relationship with the Lord. Mother and I visited churches in my quest to find a church home and be refilled with the Holy Ghost.

We visited a local church, but I did not receive a breakthrough. One Sunday we visited a large church. The music was very loud! The musicians played skillfully, and the anointing of the Lord was there. I was caught up in the anointed atmosphere. I shouted and danced in the Spirit! The Lord dealt with me. The Holy Ghost was all over me, but not in me.

I sought counsel from the clergy of the church. I needed guidance, instruction, and understanding as to how to proceed in my marriage. I did not discuss with the clergy about my experience in D.C.

The day came and for the first time ever, I fasted. I sought God for a church home. I had an overwhelming desire and longing to be in church. I desired to have relationship with the Lord again.

My heart longed for Jesus. I was seeking Him with my whole heart. I stopped by Mother's apartment. I felt an overwhelming urge to go out of the apartment. I picked up my youngest son and proceeded out of the apartment down the sidewalk towards the front of the apartment complex. I was led by the Holy Spirit across the street holding my youngest son. There were four churches on that street. I stopped by the first church and questioned the Lord if this is the one that He was trying to show me. There was no answer. I went to the next church. "Lord, is this the one?" There was no answer. I went down the street to the next church, still no answer. As I walked past the third church, my child started to cry. It was after 5 p.m. I told the Lord that it was time for my son to eat and that I did not understand what He was trying to tell me. As I turned to start back home, there were two church ladies standing at the corner. I knew that they were church ladies by the way they were dressed. I lifted my hands and started praising the Lord. With joy I hastily walked toward the ladies. When I got to them, the youngest sister stated that she had told the other sister that she knew that the Lord had turned me around. She told me that they understood what I was doing when I lifted my hands and praised the Lord. I begin to question them as to whether they were going to church. They said yes that they were going to church. They were waiting for the church bus to come. I asked them what church. Strikingly, it was the same church that we had visited that Sunday. I rejoiced and told them that I was going to run home and ask my mother to watch my children. They told me that they would keep the faith that the church bus would not come until I came back. The oldest sister is yet alive to bear witness to this story. She can testify of the validity of this area of this story. I did go to church that night. I did not receive the refilling of the Holy Ghost that night. I was refilled with the baptism of the

Holy Ghost shortly after becoming a member of the church.

Reunited with my husband, we were fruitful, and God blessed our marriage. We soon were expecting our next child. Our first daughter was a 7th month baby. My water broke early, and I went into labor. It was an extremely hard, traumatic labor. Our daughter was a premature baby. She was a low weight baby. My mother told me that after she was born, one of her lungs was not functioning properly and that she was blue at birth. Mother called the first lady of the church, and she prayed for my child's lungs to function properly. I cried at the news of hearing the state of my baby girl. I mustered up enough strength to go to the NICU where my daughter was.

When I saw our daughter for the first time, she was such a tiny little baby girl with tubes everywhere, and my heart was broken. I did not want to see our baby girl like that. I made it back to my room. I prayed and wept before the Lord and asked the Lord to give my child a miracle. God heard my prayer, and the next day when I went to see our daughter, they had removed a lot of her tubes and was feeding her with a little bottle. Thank God for prayer.

God gave us a miracle! I had to leave our baby in the hospital until she reached over five pounds in weight. I went to the hospital often to visit my baby. Upon reaching five pounds our daughter was released from the hospital. Our daughter grew. One day I noticed that one side of her face was underdeveloped. Once again, I cried unto the Lord concerning my child. I prayed and asked the Lord to make her whole and to let her face be just like the other side. Surely my Lord heard me again, and our daughter was made whole. Shortly after our first daughter was born, I conceived again. I was working at Sears and Roebuck. I began to hemorrhage. I prayed that I would not lose the baby, but I had a miscarriage.

Life went on. Aunt Evelyn came to visit from Washington, D.C. Mom brought her to visit. I came home from work that day, and Aunt Evelyn looked at me and said, "She's pregnant!" I continue to wonder how my aunt knew that I was expecting just by looking at me. I did not even know myself. Nine months later, on December 25th, 1977, Christmas Day, which fell on a Sunday, I sat in the church sanctuary. The morning service was going on, and everything was still and quiet. Suddenly, a debilitating labor pain hit me so hard. I wanted to cry out with pain, but instead I prayed a quiet prayer asking the Lord not to let me have this baby today. The pain lifted immediately. I just did not want to disrupt the service by causing a disturbance. The next day came. Sometime that day, I went into labor and had to be rushed to the hospital. God blessed me with a fine baby girl weighing in at six pounds and twelve ounces. She was healthy, and I had no complications while carrying her or after giving birth to her. My husband seemed to have a special bond with his baby girl.

When our second daughter was three months old, I conceived again. I knew right away that I had conceived. Since my pregnancies were close together, I began to hemorrhage with this one. The doctor gave me a 50/50 chance of carrying this baby to term. I was put on bed rest.

I prayed and asked God not to let me lose this baby. I asked my pastor's wife to pray also. Nine months later, God blessed us with a baby boy. I had asked the Lord to give me a son. The Lord heard me and honored my request. I had asked my husband if he wanted our first son to be junior, he said no. I wanted a junior so badly.

When this son was born, I asked my husband if I could name him Junior. He agreed. I named him Junior.

I can remember being home one day. I desired some oranges and a TV. The next thing I knew, Uncle Doug was knocking at the door. Uncle Doug had brought me a great big bag of oranges and a TV! Yes, he did. God saw the desire of my heart and honored it. I also remember desiring some roses. My husband came home with roses that day! Look at God, He will give you the desires of your heart and meet your needs.

Now we had been blessed with five children. God is good. God is good! I raised my children in church. We were very faithful Christian people because we were taught to be faithful people.

My pastor preached a strong hellfire message. We went to church four days a week. We had a special service on Saturday mornings. On Sundays, we attended Sunday School, Bible class, and Sunday night services. We kept this way of living faithfully for many years. We were taught to be faithful. We had to be obedient.

CHAPTER 8

TRAGEDY STRIKES

During one of my breakups with my husband, the children and I stayed with Mom. It was one Tuesday evening of October of 1983, during homecoming week at the church. There was an overshadowing of the Holy Ghost upon me in the bedroom at the house. I remember that tongues began to flow from my mouth like intercession.

I did not understand what this was all about, or what it meant. The presence lasted a little while and then lifted. It was close to time for evening service at the church, so we prepared ourselves and went to church. We arrived at the church and walked into the sanctuary and sat down. Shortly after taking our seats, the head lady of the usher board came to me and said that the first lady wanted to see me. I was shocked. I wondered what the matter could be. It had to be a matter of importance for the first lady to call for me. I told Mom what I had been told and ask her if she would watch the kids for me while I went to see the first lady. As I proceeded toward the first lady's office, I was met with ushers standing in the hallway with sheets draped across their arms. I was puzzled. The first lady met me, and she said to me, "Sister Linda, brace yourself! Your husband has been shot and killed!"

It took a moment to realize what I had just been told. The first lady took me into her office and questioned me as to whether the Lord had told me about this. I told her about my experience at home. We talked a little, and I went and got my mother and children to go to the hospital to see my deceased husband. I had become a widow at 29, with 5 children, ages 4 to 10 years of age. My husband and I had been married over 9 years and 10 months.

I had to accept the realization that my life would no longer include a husband. I had to accept the realization that things had changed. Life had changed. It was a new reality. It was as if I was in a bad dream. I took Valium to try to numb the pain. Nothing helped. Reality hit when I went to the funeral home to view my husband's body. I wept with tears of great sadness. He really was gone.

I had a conversation with the Lord. "But Lord, this is me! This is me, Lord!" How could this have happened to me? A young widow at 29 years old. It was so painful to have to experience the death of my husband.

I continued in widowhood for almost ten years. I worked, stayed faithful to the Lord, and raised my children with the help of the Lord Jesus Christ and my heavenly Father.

I was featured in the church magazine. I counted it an honor to be recognized for being a young widow raising five children. I was asked how I did it. I responded that the Lord had picked me up and carried me.

It was a catastrophic and life changing time in my life and the life of my children. God saw us through. My beautiful mother was always there for support and love. My brother Vincent and sister Anita and her son were there also. We lived in Garland, Texas, for a while. I had a big yellow station wagon. We often laughed and joked about being like the Brady Bunch. We were a family.

CHAPTER 9

LIFE HAPPENS

In 1992, I moved back to Dallas, Texas, and rented a house. After a while, I found favor in the eyes of the owner of the house that I rented. One day the owner of the house asked me if I would be an office manager for him. I accepted the job offer. The property owner, I will call him Mr. Harrison, bought, sold, and rented houses.

Accepting the position as office manager came with decreased rent on the house that I was renting. I would also receive bonuses if I could help with getting people to buy or lease his properties.

One day my boss hired a contractor (I will call him Tom) to restore and remodel a rundown house that he owned. The contractor and his crew remolded and performed maintenance for Mr. Harrison's houses. Tom was a good contractor and handyman.

I later found out that Tom and I both rented houses from our Mr. Harrison. I oversaw the distribution of materials that were needed for repairs and various jobs.

Tom and I worked together and became friends. Tom knew that I was a Christian woman. After a while of working together, I extended Tom an invitation to come and visit my church and to bring his family. I had decided to start keeping children to earn extra money. Tom had a young teenage daughter that I started keeping.

Soon Tom and I started dating. After a short courtship, Tom decided to ask me for my hand in marriage. I accepted.

In July 1992, we were married at the courthouse. We decided that we wanted to have a wedding ceremony and planned one. We had a full wedding ceremony! It was beautiful! We had a blended family of nine children. Tom had four children, one girl and three boys.

Having a blended family truly had its challenges.

We saw good times and bad times. Tom and I traveled a lot. For several years we celebrated by taking a trip on our anniversary day. Life was good. We enjoyed our children and raising our grandchildren.

We did family well.

Life happens. In 2002, I separated from my husband due to irreconcilable differences.

I got my divorce in 2004.

I began life as a single divorced woman and had to find life as a single lady again. It was not easy, as I had been a kept married woman living with my husband for over 10 years. Approximately two years were in separation from my spouse, for a total of nearly 12 years of marriage.

I had to go back to work, and I stayed with Mother for a while until I could get my own place. I stayed faithful to my God and lived a holy life before God and man.

CHAPTER 10

MY JOURNEY THROUGH BETHEL

The House of God

I loved being saved, being born again. I loved the new life of Christianity. Yes, the joy of the Lord is my strength. The joy that I have, the world did not give it, and the world cannot take it away. God gave me this joy. I was so grateful to be in church again, to finally have a church home, a place to come and assemble to worship the God that I serve. I was not brought up in a church. Growing up, we went to church on special holidays only. I only had vague memories of being in church with my grandmother when I was young. In my senior year of high school, I learned and memorized the 23rd Psalm. I started going to a Baptist church in the neighborhood. I had a beautiful singing voice and sang soprano in the school choir. I got in the church choir.

I cannot tell you that my experience in Bethel was one of great joy. It was not. I see my journey through Bethel as a template to prepare me for my future. 1st Thessalonians 5:18, "In everything give thanks: for this is the will of God in Christ Jesus concerning you." It prepared me for who I was to become. We have to arrive at a point in our lives where we embrace the place from whence we have come whether the experience was bad or good. Our scars are permanent reminders that we are overcomers in areas of our lives that brought us hurt and pain. I was misunderstood. I admit that not all my journey through Bethel was intolerable. There were times of love and joy. Through it all, I will interject the 91st Psalm to you, "1) He that dwelleth in the secret place of the most High shall abide under the shadow of the Almighty. 2) I will say of the Lord, he is my refuge and my fortress: my God; in him will I trust. 3) Surely he shall deliver thee from the snare of the fowler, and from the noisome pestilence."

Daniel 11:32, "and such as do wickedly against the covenant shall he corrupt by flatteries: ***but the people that know their God shall be strong and do exploits.***"

Surely my God was with me during those difficult times in my life. I had to just stand and be strong.

I would like to remember the good things that I experienced through my journey in Bethel. My first assignment was to teach Sunday School. I taught the 6-year-old boys. I also served as a substitute Sunday School teacher. I sang in various choirs and had a singing group. I sang with other singing groups. I served with the Nurses Guild for many years as I am a CNA and medical assistant. I did many years of attending Street Service and having my own Street Services. I served faithfully in the nursing home ministry for many years. I did the work of an evangelist and became a licensed minister in 2008.

CHAPTER 11

THE CALL TO GREATNESS

There were days of despair in Bethel (The House of God). One day, I was incredibly sad, and I cried and prayed to the Lord. I asked the Lord to send me a friend, someone that I could talk to and confide in.

It was lunch time. I headed to Taco Bell. I went into Taco Bell and ordered my food. As I waited for my order, I noticed a short African American lady come in. She was dressed in a warmup suit. I got my order and went to sit down to eat. The lady got her order and went to sit down to eat.

While eating my food, I heard the Holy Spirit urging me to ask her if she is single. I ignored His urging and kept eating. Once again, the Holy Spirit spoke to me and said, "Ask her if she is single." This time I acknowledged Him and asked, "Lord, how am I going to ask her if she is single like me?" I thought what kind of question is that to ask a stranger? It dawned on me that I had Gospel tracts that I used when I was witnessing and inviting people to church. I got up and went over to her and I asked her if I could give her a tract and invite her to my church. She said yes. Then I took the liberty to ask her if she was single like me. She said yes. I also asked if I could sit with her and she agreed. I sat down and introduced myself as Evangelist Linda Coleman. We began to talk about the Lord. The lady started crying. She told me that she had come to Dallas from Atlanta, Georgia. The Lord had uprooted her from all that she loved, her family, her son, grandchildren, and her home. She said she felt all alone and had just asked one of the elders at her church to pray that God would send her a strong Christian friend. She said her prayer was answered in meeting me. We both agreed that our prayers had been answered. We agreed to hang out for a while to talk and get to know one another.

We went to a nearby recreation center to walk on the indoor walking track. We spent most of the day talking and sharing stories of our lives and how God had been so good to us. This was the beginning of a beautiful and lasting friendship. Joyce (as I will call her) and I started spending time together fellowshipping and talking. I invited her to my church several times hoping she would become a member of the church.

One day Joyce invited me to attend a Wednesday night service that her church was having at the Allen Convention Center. There was nothing going on at my church, so I attended the service with Joyce. The speaker was Pastor Sheryl Brady. I had never heard her preach before that night. She was awesome! What a powerful woman of God she was! I was so impressed that I bought her DVD and decided to attend the next two service nights. Bishop T.D. Jakes preached the last night of the convention. As Bishop began to preach, it was as though he was speaking directly to me in my situation. These three nights at the convention center in Allen changed my life and gave me a new perspective. The messages that came forth that night help me to realize that everything that I had gone through at the House of Bethel was designed to prepare me for my destiny.

The time for change had come in my life. It was time to move on. I started visiting The Potter's House of Dallas.

My big sister, Joyce, was my support and best friend. She held my hand as I made the transition in my new journey at the Potter's House of Dallas. In June of 2011, I was blessed to become a member.

I was able to be restored as a licensed minister. I serve in the hospital ministry, nursing home ministry, and I am an active member of the Silver Team. I served with the singles' ministry. I was recommended for eldership. I attended the Potter's House School of Ministry and became an ordained elder in June of 2017.

In February of 2020, the Lord told me to start a Sisterhood Group. The Women of Purpose and Destiny Sisterhood came about. I am presently serving in the T.O.R.I. Ministry as a mentor to women coming out of prison.

I am so grateful to my great pastor Bishop T. D. Jakes for seeking God for the flock of God and the needs of

His sheep. I have been fed quite well and have grown greatly under this ministry. I soar in accomplishments and I am on my way to great heights and depths in Christ Jesus. I am happy! Thank you, heavenly Father, sweet Lord Jesus!

CONCLUSION

THE MANDATE FROM THE LORD

April 30th, 2014, I sustained a concussion. My sister and I had met at the assisted living facility where our mother lived. We went out to take care of some business. When we arrived at our destination, we decided to put our purses in the trunk of my sister's car. After we had finished taking care of our business, we went back to our mother's place. I had left my car there and rode with my sister in her car. Upon arriving at the facility, I told my sister to pop the trunk of her car. I got out of her car and went to the trunk to retrieve my purse. When I looked in the back of the trunk of the car, my purse was far back in the trunk. I reached in deeply into the trunk to retrieve my purse. As I came up out of the trunk of the car, the lower end of trunk of the car came down with great pressure and hit me across my forehead. I was stunned and in pain. A hematoma arose immediately on my forehead. It was as though someone had pushed the trunk of the car down on my forehead with great pressure. I thought to myself, "Oh my God! What just happened? How did this happen?" There was no one there or near to have caused this to have happened. There was no great wind blowing. I never told my sister what happened to me. I just retrieved my purse, got in my car, and headed home. After arriving home, the hematoma had subsided. I prepared for bed and went to sleep. I did not put an ice pack on my forehead, nor did I seek medical attention.

The Lord was gracious to me and spared my life. Thank you, Lord Jesus.

The Lord awakened me the next day. I was a professional bus operator driving for a school district. I did not go to work that morning.

I was experiencing some shoulder and neck pain and decided to stay home and rest.

I went to work feeling fine for the evening shift.

There was no pain or indication of a head injury. Upon arriving to work, I clocked in and retrieved my key to the bus from the dispatcher. I started walking toward the bus and could not make it. I did not have enough strength to make it to the bus. I had to stop, rest, and regroup until I was able to continue walking toward the bus. I made it to the bus but realized that I was incapable of driving it. I managed to go back to the dispatch office. I told the dispatcher that the night prior I had been hit in the head by the trunk of the car. I was told to go to the ER. By the grace of God, slowly but surely, I was able to drive from my job all the way to a hospital in Dallas. I struggled to get from my car to the ER. I told them that I had been hit in the head by the trunk of a car. I was seen immediately. I became incapacitated and was rushed into a hospital room where I lost strength and was admitted to the hospital. I had sustained a concussion. I was in the hospital for two days. I was dismissed to go home after the two-day inpatient hospital stay.

Shortly after arriving home to recover, the Lord spoke to me. He said, "Write."

I knew that I had a book in me. I had started writing sometime before but became lackadaisical. The Lord had had enough of my laziness and put a mandate on my life to write this book. I was off work for six weeks and under the doctor's care with this concussion. The events and details of this book are true. This is my story. All glory goes to the Lord and God of my life. There are people living today that can validate the authenticity of this writing.

Here is your book, Lord. I surrender all.

I deliver my soul. Amen!

ACKNOWLEDGEMENTS

Proverbs 3:6, "In all thy ways acknowledge him, and he shall direct thy paths."

Thank you, heavenly Father, Lord Jesus Christ, for divine inspiration and direction in the composition of this book. My story, your book. All glory belongs to you, Lord. I surrender all.

I am ever thankful to my wonderful parents, William and Antionette, for giving me love and care in my upbringing.

My beautiful mother, Antoinette Coleman, who was a rock and jewel. Mom, you were the rock and symbol of strength, a virtuous woman, who held her house together well. She taught us, and instilled in her children strength, love, and dignity. She ruled with a strong hand and always said, "I have good children!"

Thank God for my brother Vincent and sister Anita, and my daughters Yvette and Hadeshia for being supportive and willing. Thank God for my children. Thank you, cousin Brenda for being with me from the beginning, during my conversion time to this present time. Thanks for being the family historian.

Thank you to my beautiful Aunts Edna, Deloris, Phyllis, Glenda, and Uncle James, aka Uncle Jimmy. You are some of the most beautiful people I know and have always been supportive to me and my siblings. You are the essence of what family is supposed to be. Thank God for the upbringing of your parents that continue to remain firm to this day. Your parents, Levi and Marie, would be immensely proud of you all.

A special thanks to all the pastors, bishops, teachers, elders, and others that taught me, raised me, and instilled God's Word in me to help me grow, mature, and become who I am today. Thank you, Bishop T. D. Jakes, for feeding me well the engrafted Word of God from the table of the

Lord that made me fat in the Lord. I have grown immensely.

Thank you to my college teacher, professor Kennon Brownlee. My friend and confidant. Thank you for your expertise, wisdom, and guidance.

Thank you, Elder Wayne Morris, teacher, instructor, friend, and confidant. You have been there for me during the difficult times of my life. Thank you for being my spiritual warfare teacher. Thank you for covering me and my family. Fighting for us and covering us in the most needed times.

To Elder Carla Carter. My friend and sister. You always see the best in me. I have nothing but good to say about you.

I thank God for excellent leaders in ministry. Leaders of the Silver Team, Elders Jaimie and Jo Patterson, Elder Brixie Gatlin, who supported me and prayed with me and my family during sickness, bereavement, and loss. Thanks to Elder Jan Green for support.

Thank you, cousin, Pastor Brien Robinson for being a support in my life.

Thanks to all family members, church members, friends, and everyone that helped me during my journey. I pray God's blessings upon you and yours.

In Loving Memory
The Essence of You!

To my loving parents William and Antoinette Coleman. My loving grandparents, Clarence and Odessa Williams. Levi and Marie Coleman. My baby brother Dwight Coleman. My beautiful aunts, Wilma Williams, Evelyn Allen, Velma Faye Ware, Vera Coleman Tyler, Uncle Nova Joe and Helen Williams, Clarence and Shirley Williams. My uncles Douglass Ware, Morris Allen, Clarence Coleman, Melvin Coleman. Cousins: Beverly Williams, Tommie Jackson, Willard J. Williams, Shelia Jackson, that have passed on before me. To my husband and son; Rickey Glenn Thompson, Sr. and Rickey Glenn Thompson, Jr. Great grand twin baby Gilanna Thompson.

I am the fabric of you. You are the hands and thread that seamed me together. You are the hands that molded, shaped, and made me. You covered and protected me. You showed and taught me love. You instilled in me strength and quality. You gave me joy, happiness, and peace. You are the essence of who I am, have become, and am becoming. I love you.

All of you have sown greatly into my life in one way or another, I am who I am and have become today because of you. I love and miss you. I journey on to make Heaven my home.

Linda Coleman

ABOUT THE AUTHOR

Linda Coleman is a seasoned woman of God, having accepted the Lord Jesus Christ as Savior in October 1975. When she was a child, Linda lived with her family—her parents William and Antionette Coleman, her grandmother Odessa Woods, and her baby brother Vincent Coleman—in South Dallas, TX.

After the death of her maternal grandmother, Linda's family lived for a few years in San Antonio, TX. Linda was educated in Dallas and San Antonio.

She is an achiever. Early in life, Linda learned that to accomplish things, she needed determination, drive, and a lot of courage. She had to learn to be purpose-driven.

After relocating to Dallas, she found her life unfolding in ways that led to great disappointment, turmoil, and anguish.

Linda experienced failed relationships and a disappointing marriage. However, this led to a turn of events that resulted in her accepting the Lord Jesus Christ as Savior. She received salvation and the infilling of the

Holy Ghost in the D.C. apartment of her aunt, Evelyn Allen. Linda's lack of a Christian upbringing challenged her as she went through the process of becoming a born-again child of God. She knew nothing about the Holy Ghost and backslid after her initial infilling of this divine gift. Linda became a member of a local church, where she received her license as a minister in 2008. She graduated from Roosevelt High School as part of the class of 1972. There, she was a member of the National Honor Society. After high school, she attended El Centro College.

In 1987, Linda attended a local school and received her certificate as a Certified Nurse Aide.

Also, Linda attended Education America (currently Remington College), where she studied Medical Assisting and received her diploma in 2001. After 32-plus years, she retired from being a Certified Nurse Aide in December 2019. Linda has a CDL, which she attained in 2014, and continues to work as a professional school bus driver for First Student Transportation Company, serving the Irving School District. She is currently a member of The Potter's House Church of Dallas, where Bishop T. D. Jakes is pastor.

She has been an active member of the church since 2011. Linda attended The Potter's House School of Ministry and became an ordained elder of the church in June 2017. Linda's passion is ministry. Over the years, she has faithfully served in many areas in the Holiness Church. She was a Sunday School teacher, Nursing Home Ministry leader, and member of various choirs and singing groups. She has a beautiful singing voice.

Linda served faithfully in the Nurses Guild at church for many years. She and other avid soldiers of the Cross held and participated in Street Service for years.

She is an active member of the Silver Team at The Potter's House, the Hospital/Nursing Home Ministries, and the Bishop's Choir. She served in the Single's Ministry, Evangelism Ministry, and Spiritual Warfare Ministry. Linda has a ministry to help women who are hurting. She has a compassionate soul and spirit.

Currently, with the T.O.R.I. Ministry of The Potter's House of Dallas, Linda serves as a mentor to women coming out of prison. This ministry is extremely rewarding to her and helps her to be her best self. Linda is empathetic, loving, kind, and caring. She imparts the wisdom of her age and experience to the ladies. Linda has found that she does not have to look for ministry. If the good Lord wakes her up, ministry finds her!

In February 2020, the Lord impressed upon Linda the need to start a sisterhood group. The group "Women of Purpose and Destiny" met for the first time at Luby's Cafeteria in DeSoto, TX. The ladies loved the sisterhood group and were so blessed to be a part of it!

Linda experienced great heartache in the church. However, she does not blame God for what man does. Linda has often heard that it is not the church that hurts you but some of the people in the church.

'It ain't what they call you, it's what you answer to.
— WC Fields.

Linda's ability to embrace change brought about great victory in her life.

"Now thanks be unto God, which always causes us to triumph in Christ, and maketh manifest the savior of his knowledge by us in every place," 2 Corinthians 2:14-16.

Index

CPSIA information can be obtained
at www.ICGtesting.com
Printed in the USA
BVHW040934170821
614608BV00018B/547